WANT TO BE A
NASCAR Driver?

By Bob Woods

The
Child's
World®
www.childsworld.com

Published in the United States of America by
The Child's World®
1980 Lookout Drive • Mankato, MN 56003-1705
800-599-READ • www.childsworld.com

ACKNOWLEDGMENTS

The Child's World®:
Mary Berendes, Publishing Director

Produced by Shoreline Publishing Group LLC
President / Editorial Director: James Buckley, Jr.
Designer: Tom Carling, carlingdesign.com
Assistant Editor: Jim Gigliotti

Photo Credits:
Cover: Getty Images.
Interior: AP/Wide World 1, 4, 9, 10, 14, 17, 24, 27,
28; Reuters: 6; Joe Robbins: 2, 12, 16, 18, 21, 23,
26, 29.

**LIBRARY OF CONGRESS
CATALOGING-IN-PUBLICATION DATA**

Woods, Bob.
  Want to be a NASCAR driver? / by Bob Woods.
    p. cm. — (The world of NASCAR)
  Includes bibliographical references and index.
  ISBN 978-1-60253-084-3 (library bound : alk.
paper)
  1. Stock car racing—United States—Juvenile
literature. 2.   Stock car drivers—United States—
Juvenile literature. 3. NASCAR (Association)—
Juvenile literature. I. Title.
  GV1029.9.S74W69 2008
  796.72023—dc22
                                      2007049084

Contents

[OPPOSITE]
*Would you like to be in this NASCAR race
(instead of just looking at a picture)? Find
out how to "earn a ride" inside.*

So, You Want to Be a NASCAR Driver?

THERE'S A LOT MORE TO BECOMING A NASCAR driver than puttin' the pedal to the metal. Sure, racing team owners are looking for men and women who can drive real fast. But drivers also need a good understanding of the entire car. They need to communicate with the **crew chief** and the rest of the race team. They need to be physically fit to handle a 3,400-pound (1,542-kg) road rocket. They need to be mentally tough to handle tight racing in a pack of 43 cars.

That's just life on the track. Off it, drivers have to deal with the **media** and the fans. They have to keep their **sponsors** happy. They have to find quality time for their families and friends.

It takes tons of hard work, determination, and dedication to reach the NASCAR finish line. Just ask Kyle Busch. He raced go-karts when he was a kid. Then he spent many years racing other cars before he was ready for stock cars. And along the way, he graduated from high school a full year early with honors. It all paid off in 2005, however, when Kyle became NASCAR's **Rookie** of the Year and won his first Cup Series race.

NASCAR welcomes a fresh crop of rookie drivers every year. Let's look at what it takes to become one of those winners.

[OPPOSITE]
Before he could climb into a NASCAR vehicle, Kyle Busch had to face many challenges.

5

From Go-Karts to Stock Cars

MOST KIDS ARE THRILLED IF THEY CAN RIDE A bicycle by the time they're six years old. Apparently, a two-wheeler wasn't quite thrilling enough for young Kyle Busch while growing up in Las Vegas, Nevada. He was just six the first time he got behind the wheel of a go-kart. Before long, he and his older brother Kurt were racing go-karts. Neither of the Busch brothers has slowed down since then. In fact, they both went on to become NASCAR drivers!

In 2005, Kyle was 19 and racing stock cars. That year, he became NASCAR's Nextel Cup Rookie of the Year. The Nextel Cup now is called the Sprint Cup. It is the major league of NASCAR, the top level that every driver wants to reach. Kyle earned his award by winning two races and finishing in the top five in seven others. He got his first big win when he took the **checkered flag** at

[OPPOSITE]
Go-karts are a great way to start enjoying high-speed racing action.

the Sony HD 500 on September 4, 2005. He won again in November at the Checker Auto Parts 500.

It was a long road that finally led to Kyle's spectacular rookie season in 2005. And it all began with go-karts. In fact, many of today's NASCAR drivers started out the same way. Kevin Harvick, the 2001 Rookie of the Year, got a go-kart as a kindergarten "graduation" present. Over the next 10 years, he became a big-time winner on the go-kart circuit. Jamie McMurray raced go-karts nationally

Little Cars, Big Fun

It's easy to see why so many future NASCAR drivers race go-karts first. They are inexpensive and easy to maintain. A go-kart is basically a lawnmower engine bolted to a sturdy metal **chassis** [CHASS-ee]. However, they can be serious racing machines. The engines range from 5 to 40 **horsepower**, depending on the level of competition. Go-karts can weigh up to about 300 pounds (136 kg) and reach speeds up to 120 miles (193 km) per hour. Therefore, go-karts, and the drivers who race them, are required to follow strict rules about safety equipment and clothing.

Races are held on both short oval tracks and twisty road courses. Young drivers learn basic turning, braking, and **accelerating** skills. The World Kart Association, formed in 1971, organizes most official go-kart races in the United States. Races are held nearly every weekend all across the country. They even race go-karts at the famous Daytona International Speedway in Florida, home of NASCAR's biggest annual race, the Daytona 500.

and internationally from ages 8 to 17. He won four U.S. Go-Kart titles and one World Go-Kart Championship. Jeff Gordon, Ricky Rudd, and 2002 and 2005 NASCAR Cup Champion Tony Stewart got their first taste of racing behind a go-kart wheel, too.

Young Kyle learned more than just how to drive his go-kart. His father was a stock-car driver, too, and was always tinkering with race cars in the family garage. He taught both Kurt and Kyle the inner workings of engines, brakes, and other moving parts of a car. By the time he was 10, Kyle knew so much about auto mechanics, he served as the crew chief for Kurt at races.

Along with learning from his family, Kyle got pointers from the best: two-time NASCAR champion Jimmie Johnson (left).

"Racing has always been in our family," says Kurt, who is seven years older than Kyle. The brothers share happy memories of regularly going to a local track for Friday-night races. "Once you have that racing bug, you can't get rid of it," Kyle admits.

Kyle launched his own competitive racing career when he was 13. Like Kurt, he raced dwarf cars.

Dwarf cars are 5/8-scale replicas of older American automobiles, built between the 1920s and 1940s, which were the original stock car racers. Dwarf cars have full steel roll cages, sheet-metal bodies, and are powered by four-cylinder motorcycle engines between 750cc and 1200cc. They can reach speeds of more than 100 miles (161 km) per hour on straightaways.

Kyle eventually moved up to racing legend cars, which are similar to dwarf cars, only more powerful. From 1999–2001, Kyle won more than 65 legend car races and two track championships while competing at the "Bullring" at Las Vegas Motor Speedway. On that same, paved oval track—just 3/8 of a mile (.6 km) long—Kyle also raced stock cars for the first time. Called Late Models, they are not quite a big and powerful as those on the NASCAR Sprint Cup circuit. Kyle quickly got the hang of driving his. In 2001 alone, he celebrated 10 Late Model victories at the Bullring.

Kyle's success at every level of racing caught the attention of Jack Roush, the owner of Roush Racing in North Carolina. Kyle was just 16 and a junior in high school when Roush Racing hired him to drive a souped-up pickup truck in the NASCAR Craftsman Truck Series in 2001. He finished ninth in his very first race. After that first taste of NASCAR competition, Kyle was hungry for more. His dream would come true before too long.

Until 1982, NASCAR had a national Late-Model Sportsman Division that held races all over the country. Today, it's called the Nationwide Series.

Driving Up the Ladder

RICK HENDRICK OWNS A GROUP OF SUCCESSFUL
NASCAR racing teams. Since he formed Hendrick
Motorsports in North Carolina in 1984, Rick's teams
have won seven Cup Series championships and three
Craftsman Truck Series titles. His top drivers include four-
time Cup Series champion Jeff Gordon (1995, 1997,
1998, 2001) and Jimmie Johnson. Jimmie was the 2006
and 2007 Cup Series champion. Rick and other team
owners are always looking for talented new drivers. Not
just anyone will do, though. NASCAR drivers have to be
the cream of the stock-car crop.

As in any sport, there are many levels in stock car
racing. There are amateur drivers who race just as a
fun hobby. At the top are the pros who race for years
and dream of making it to NASCAR's top level. Since
before NASCAR was founded in 1948, there have been
hundreds of small dirt and paved tracks built all over
the country. Drivers haul their race cars to a local track
on weekend nights, pay the entry fee, and wait for the
green flag to drop at the start of the race. Most of these
"weekend warriors" don't have organized teams or
sponsors to pay for cars, engines, and crews.

Some of those drivers stick with it and become
really good. They race faster, harder, and smarter than

[OPPOSITE]
*Rick Hendrick had
to watch a lot of
races and meet a lot
of people before he
chose a driver. He
picked a good one;
Jimmie Johnson (right)
won NASCAR titles in
2006 and 2007.*

their competitors. Their cars run better. They take lots of checkered flags. You might say they were born to race. But they've also worked very hard at it for years. Those are the drivers that owners like Rick Hendrick try to find.

Rick's eyes lit up when Kyle Busch's name was mentioned in early 2003. Kyle was still just 17 years old, but on the racetrack he already was known as an experienced winner. After Kyle competed in the Craftsman Truck Series in 2001, NASCAR made a new rule that drivers in any of its three major series had to be at least 18. So in 2002 Kyle raced stock cars on the American Speed Association (ASA) circuit. In 20 races, he posted five top-five and 10 top-10 finishes. On February 4, 2003, a few months before his 18th birthday, Kyle signed a multi-year contract to race for Hendrick Motorsports.

"Kyle is one of the best young racers I've ever been around, and it's certainly exciting to have him on board," Hendrick said at the time.

Kyle turned 18 on May 2. Three weeks later, he competed in his first NASCAR Busch Series race and finished in second place. (The Busch Series is now called the Nationwide Series. Its cars are a bit lighter and less powerful than the cars in the Sprint Cup.)

How did Kyle get Number 5? NASCAR numbers are assigned to the race team, not the driver. Roush Racing controls Number 5, and the team chose Kyle as the driver to make it famous!

ABCs of Stock Car Racing

It's hard for any newcomer to jump right into the tough Sprint Cup circuit, where the world's best cars and drivers race. So many stock car drivers—including Kyle Busch—take the "ABC" route from the minor leagues to the majors.

They begin by competing in ARCA (Automobile Racing Club of America) events. Some are held at Daytona, Talladega, Atlanta, and other tracks where NASCAR runs. The next step is NASCAR's Busch Series (now known as Nationwide . . . so it must be "ANC" now). Pass the test there, and you're ready for Cup racing. In 2004, Kyle's stock car education included ARCA races, Busch races, and Cup races—ABC.

As he prepared to compete in all 34 Busch Series races in 2004, Kyle knew that doing well would take a team effort. Even the best driver needs good mechanics to keep his car running tip-top for every race. Then once he's zooming around the track, his pit crew has to change the car's tires and fill the gas tank in just seconds. "It's a matter of getting everyone working together so you can be successful," Kyle explains.

No, that's not NASCAR champ Jimmie Johnson with another number. Fellow Roush Racing driver Kyle Busch had Johson's familiar sponsor on his own Busch Series car in 2004.

It also helped that Kyle had an older brother to serve as a teacher and role model.

"I've learned a lot of driving abilities from him," Kyle says of Kurt, who won the 2004 Cup Series

championship. "On and off the track, he's been the greatest that I've seen."

Kyle didn't do too badly himself in 2004. He drove away with five checkered flags and 16 top-five and 22 top-10 finishes. That was plenty to earn him Rookie of the Year honors in the Busch Series and put him in second place for the championship.

Hendrick decided Kyle was ready to test his skills at the NASCAR's top level. Kyle started six Cup races in 2004, but didn't do nearly as well as in the Busch events. He only finished two Cup races, and three ended early when he crashed. Kyle did much better, though, in 2005. Driving the No. 5 car, he competed in all 36 Cup Series races. He posted two wins and nine top-five finishes. He had 13 top-10 finishes. No other newcomer to the Cup Series did better, so Kyle was named the Rookie of the Year.

Team owner Rick Hendrick and driver Kyle Busch team up off the track, too. Here, they're donating money to one of the many charities NASCAR supports.

Getting an Off-the-Track Education

FINALLY MAKING IT TO THE BIG-TIME WORLD OF
NASCAR Sprint Cup racing is a dream come true. It is
also an adjustment for new drivers. The competition is
tougher than in the minor races. All the drivers, cars,
and crews are the best of the best. The pressure to win
races—and money—is greater. The schedule is longer,
with events held almost every weekend from February
to November. And in between races, drivers have to test
new engines, tires, and car setups. There are practice
runs and qualifying events for **pole position**.

Drivers keep busy off the track, too. It costs about
$12 million a year to operate a Sprint Cup team. Much of
that money is spent on car chassis and bodies, engines,
and parts. The team owner has to pay mechanics,
engineers, and pit crews for their work. There are offices,
garages, tools, hauling trucks, and other equipment. It's
expensive for the team to travel from city to city, stay in
hotels, and eat.

A big part of an owner's job is to get money from
sponsors to cover the team's costs. Sponsors are
companies that contribute money. In return, their **logos**
are placed on cars and drivers' uniforms. Sponsors
include companies that manufacture the stock cars.
These are Chevrolet, Dodge, Ford, and Toyota. Each team

[OPPOSITE]
Kurt (left) and Kyle
Busch are one of
many brother pairs
to succeed in NASCAR.
Other brother
pairs include the
Labontes, the
Wallaces, the Bodines,
and the Allisons.

Learning to Communicate

NASCAR has become one of the most popular sports in America. Because of that, NASCAR gets lots of media attention—TV, radio, Web sites, magazines, newspapers, and books. That means the drivers have to be available for interviews, film and video tapings, and photographs. They also have to find time to mingle with fans at the track and sign autographs.

"It's nice to have fans out there who collect your souvenirs and support your team," says Kyle, who left Hendrick Motorsports after the 2007 season and began driving the No. 18 car for Joe Gibbs Racing in 2008.

also has a main company sponsor, plus other sponsors who contribute less than the main sponsor. Take a look at the logos on a Sprint Cup car, and you'll get the picture.

Being a NASCAR sponsor is one way those companies sell their products and services. In return, the drivers star in advertisements and make public appearances for their sponsors. "All the work in going to appearances and meeting with sponsors can be time-consuming," admits Ryan Newman, whose No. 12 car is sponsored by oil maker Mobil 1.

Besides being celebrities, drivers are athletes, too. Some people say that NASCAR drivers aren't really athletes like those who play baseball, football, basketball, soccer, and other sports. NASCAR fans and drivers will tell you that that's not true. You really do have to be physically fit to drive a race car. You need arm strength to steer the car at high speeds for up to five hours. All the shifting and braking is almost like jogging. And on a hot afternoon, it can reach 140 degrees F (60 degrees C) inside the car!

"Being physically fit and able to recover quickly is very important," says Robby Gordon, who drives the No. 7 car. He does **cardiovascular** exercises to help his heart and breathing. Kyle Busch does stretching exercises before a race to keep himself flexible and alert. Two-time Cup Series champ Jimmie Johnson spends a lot of time between seasons riding his mountain bike to stay in shape. All that is just one more part of a NASCAR driver's busy life.

Meeting with fans and signing autographs is part of a driver's life—as Kasey Kahne learns here.

All That Hard Work Pays Off

JAMIE MCMURRAY HAD BEEN A BIG WINNER in go-kart racing. When he was 17 years old, he switched to stock cars. He dominated the short tracks near his hometown of Joplin, Missouri. His winning ways continued at the I-44 and Lakeside Speedways in the Kansas City area. Jamie's luck seemed to run out, however, when he moved up to NASCAR's minor leagues. He had never won in 65 career starts in the Busch Series or in 17 starts in NASCAR's Craftsman Truck Series. That's one reason why his win in the UAW-GM Quality 500 in October 2002 was so stunning. The other was that it was only his second Cup Series race ever.

So how did Jamie get a Cup Series "ride," anyway? Aren't owners and sponsors looking for proven winners? "For people who didn't know me, it seemed like I came out of nowhere," Jamie says. NASCAR team owners Chip

Ganassi and Felix Sabates knew who he was, though. "I had been a fan of Jamie's for a long time," says Sabates. He had watched a lot of Jamie's races on TV. "I liked his style of driving. He's smart."

The owners had hired Jamie to race one of their Cup Series cars beginning in 2003. But when their veteran driver, Sterling Marlin, was injured in a crash, they picked Jamie to replace him for the rest of the 2002 season. He finished 26th in his first Cup race. Then he shocked everyone a week later at Lowe's Motor Speedway in North Carolina. In the final laps, he outraced veteran

Kevin Harvick had big shoes to fill, taking over for legendary driver Dale Earnhardt Sr. But car owner Richard Childress (right) knew he had another winner on his racing team.

drivers Bobby Labonte, Tony Stewart, and Jeff Gordon to the finish line. He set a new NASCAR modern-era record for a driver getting his first win the earliest in a career. Jamie would go on to become the 2003 Cup Series Rookie of the Year.

Taking that first Cup Series checkered flag is a dream come true for drivers. They race many miles and wait many years for that special moment.

"Racing is something I've wanted to do my whole life," says Kevin Harvick.

Kevin raced as a kid, all the way through high school. He left college in 1997 to become a full-time stock car driver. Kevin did well in NASCAR's minor series. After Dale Earnhardt Sr.'s tragic death at the 2001 Daytona 500, team owner Richard Childress chose Kevin to take his place. In just his third start, in the Cracker Barrel 500 in Atlanta, Kevin won.

Even with Kevin and Jamie's rapid success, rookies didn't always win so quickly. Tony Stewart, the 2002 Cup Series champion, was a newcomer in 1999. He took his first checkered flag in his 25th start. Yet Tony was the first rookie to win in NASCAR's top division since the late Davey Allison won at Talladega in 1987, his 14th start. It took Dale Earnhardt Jr. 14 starts, too, and his famous father 16 starts. Stewart went on to set a rookie record that year with three race victories.

These days, Kevin works to support young drivers by owning his own racing team. Cars from Kevin Harvick, Inc. race in the Nationwide and Craftsman Truck Series.

Sometimes, drivers race completely different types of cars before switching to NASCAR. Several have started out racing "open-wheel" (no fenders over the wheels) cars in Formula One or Indy Racing League events. Open-wheel cars are smaller, lighter, and faster than stock cars. But drivers still learn the skills needed to race a stock car. Past open-wheel champions who crossed over to NASCAR include Mario Andretti and A.J. Foyt, who both won the Daytona 500. In 2007, former open-wheel star Juan Pablo Montoya was NASCAR's rookie of the year.

Juan Pablo Montoya drove cars like this one in Formula 1 on his way to becoming an Indy 500 winner.

Kid Kyle Comes Through in California

Kyle Busch scored his first NASCAR Cup Series victory in a tense race on September 4, 2005, at California Speedway in Fontana, California. Leading on the final lap, Kyle had Greg Biffle right alongside his No. 5 Kellogg's Chevrolet. Kyle hung tough, though, and crossed the finish line just .554 seconds ahead of Greg. That's less time than it takes you to snap your finger! And just like that, Kyle also became the youngest driver ever to win a Cup Series race. He was just 20 years old.

"A lot of the older guys don't like it when you come in and run well and win a race at such a young age," Kyle told reporters after the race. "But owners want young drivers because they can mold them. Older guys are set in their ways; drivers like me aren't."

Juan's success in open-wheel racing includes winning the famous Indianapolis 500 in 2000. In 2007, he had a full-time "ride" with NASCAR's Chip Ganassi Racing team, driving the No. 42 Texaco/Havoline car. Juan celebrated his first Cup Series victory on June 24 when he took the checkered flag in the Toyota/Save Mart 350 at Infineon Raceway in Sonoma, California.

In his new "ride," Montoya has a roof over his head! He also has a new crew of experts helping him on the road to a NASCAR championship.

"It's the biggest thing I've done in my racing career," Juan admitted afterward.

No matter how they get there, talented drivers are always hoping for their first visit to NASCAR's Victory Lane. They're racking up valuable seat time in the minors. They're communicating well with crews. They're learning to understand their high-tech cars. They're keeping sponsors and fans happy. And like the owners who hire them, they want to win.

Stages of Racing

Here are typical steps, from beginning to end, that drivers move through to make it to Sprint Cup racing:

➤ Go-karts

➤ Quarter-midget cars

➤ Midgets

➤ Sprints

➤ Dwarf and Legend cars

➤ Late-model stock cars

➤ United States Auto Club (USAC)

➤ Automobile Racing Club of America (ARCA)

➤ NASCAR Craftsman Truck Series

➤ NASCAR Nationwide Series

➤ NASCAR Sprint Cup Series (pictured)

Glossary

accelerating   increasing speed

cardiovascular   having to do with the heart and lungs

chassis   the metal skeleton or framework of a car

checkered flag   the flag that signifies the winning car has crossed the finish line

crew chief   the person in charge of the members of a NASCAR race team

horsepower   a measure of engine strength

logos   symbols that represent companies or teams

media   people who work for TV, radio, newspaper, or Internet companies that report news

pole position   the best starting spot—the inside of the front row

rookie   an athlete in his or her first sports season

sponsors   companies that pay an athlete or a team to promote their product

Find Out More

BOOKS

Dirt Track Daredevils: The History of NASCAR
By Bob Woods
Tradition Books, 2002
Meet the people who zoomed to NASCAR success and discover the often-bumpy roads they drove to glory.

Eyewitness NASCAR
By James Buckley Jr.
DK Publishing, 2005
This photo-filled book takes you inside the world of NASCAR. See close-up pictures of engines and other gear, meet the heroes of the sport, and see more photos of pit-stop and racing action.

NASCAR
By Rachel Eagen
Crabtree Publishing, 2006
Take a green- to checkered-flag look at NASCAR to find out more about the world that young drivers long to join.

NASCAR in the Driver's Seat
By Mike Kennedy and Mark Stewart
Lerner Publications, 2007
Climb behind the wheel and experience what a NASCAR driver feels during a race—plus find out how drivers train to be their best.

NASCAR Record & Fact Book
Sporting News Books, 2008
This handy reference source is loaded with facts and figures about current drivers and NASCAR history.

WEB SITES

Visit our Web site for lots of links about NASCAR:
www.childsworld.com/links

Note to Parents, Teachers, and Librarians: We routinely check our Web links to make sure they're safe, active sites—so encourage your readers to check them out!

Index

ABOUT THE AUTHOR

Bob Woods is a writer who lives in Connecticut. He has written many books and magazine articles about motor sports, and was the editor of the Harley-Davidson motorcycle company's 100th anniversary magazine.